The Little Guide to Unprocrastination

The Little Guide to Unprocrastination

Leo Babauta

WAKING LION PRESS

ISBN 978-1-4341-0350-5

Waking Lion Press™, the Waking Lion Press logo, and The Editorium™ are trademarks of The Editorium, LLC

The Editorium, LLC
West Valley City, UT 84128-3917
wakinglionpress.com
wakinglion@editorium.com

Contents

About this Book

This is a Little Guide. It's not meant to be long—just about every chapter is very short. You'll get the basics of everyone's favorite problem—Procrastination—and then my time-proven methods for beating that problem.

A few key concepts are pounded home enough times that you won't be able to miss the message.

Then you'll quickly be done reading, and be on your way to get amazing things done.

This book is Uncopyrighted, and written by Leo Babauta of *Zen Habits*. Read more about me in the chapter about My Procrastination Story, and even more at *LeoBabauta.com*.

The Irony—You'll Read This Later!

Let's start with everyone's favorite procrastination jokes about a procrastination book, just to get them out of the way:

I know I should buy this book but I'll buy it later!

I'll read it tomorrow! Hahahaha!

I keep meaning to get around to beating procrastination, but . . .

OK, that's out of the way.

Seriously, though, if you're a major procrastinator, you might just want to kick the procrastination habit but instead you keep putting it off. The reason is probably Fear.

If you do nothing else, skip to the chapter on Fear. At least if you procrastinate after that, you'll know why.

My Un-Procrastination Story

Hi my friends. I'm Leo Babauta, creator of *Zen Habits* and *mnmlist.com,* and author of the books *Focus,* and *The Power of Less.*

I'm a habitual procrastinator. It's something I've struggled with my entire life, just like almost anyone else. It's something we all deal with, to greater or lesser degrees. I'm no exception.

In school I procrastinated so much I never did homework and despite great test grades (I always crammed the night before), I got mediocre grades. I did well in the newspaper industry and in politics, but I always did things at the last minute and barely pulled them off.

I had a million things I wanted to achieve in life, and yet I never got around to starting them.

Sound familiar? If you're a chronic procrastinator too, this book is for you.

In 2006 I found some solutions after repeated (failed) attempts to conquer the problem. In 2007 I discovered my passion and my productivity took off. I finally beat procrastination!

Truth be told, I still procrastinate sometimes. I get stuck on the Internet like anyone else. But I still get the important things done, and that's what matters.

Using the simple methods in this book, here's just a sample of what I've done:

Created *Zen Habits,* one of the Top 25 blogs according to TIME magazine, and have run it successfully for four years (as of this writing in 2011).

Wrote and published several books in the last three years: *The Power of Less, Focus, Zen To Done, The Simple Guide to a Minimalist Life,* and more.

Wrote (but decided not to publish) two novels during two separate *NaNoWriMo* bouts, including one where I wrote over 110,000 words in a month.

Created two other successful blogs: *Write To Done* and *mnmlist,* each with well over 10,000 subscribers.

Ran several marathons and a couple triathlons.

Co-created a successful business (with a fantastic partner, Mary Jaksch): *A-List Blogging Bootcamps.*

I wrote this book in three days.

I did all of this, of course, with six kids and a wife. If I can do this with six kids, you have no excuses.

How I did all this isn't complicated. I followed the simple principles in this book. I'm sharing them with you here in hopes that you'll finally beat procrastination too—and go on to do the things you've always wanted to do.

Why Procrastination Hurts Us

What's so bad about procrastination? Honestly, procrastination isn't all bad—see the next chapter, When Procrastination is Good. I enjoy it as much as the next guy.

But it can hurt us, which is why I've written this book.

Some of the ways procrastination hurts us:

It can stop us from getting our work done, hurting our performance at work.

Even if we get the work done, we often do it rushed, or don't put everything we have into the job, resulting in sub standard results.

It can cause us to take longer than necessary, making us work longer and cutting into other things we want to spend time on—like exercise, hobbies, relaxing, and time with family.

It's a waste of the precious few hours we have on this Earth.

It increases stress levels—we think about what we're not doing when we're not doing it.

It can prevent us from achieving our goals.

It can hurt our self-esteem. When you procrastinate long enough, you begin to believe you are lazy, incompetent, undisciplined, maybe a loser. It can be difficult to stop yourself once you slide down this slope.

It can prevent us from ever going after our dreams.

The last two items are the worst, in my opinion. If you read this book for no other reason, do it because you want to get off your butt and start going after your dreams.

When Procrastination is Good

It is the Puritanical nature of our culture (if you're from the U.S.) that portrays procrastination as an evil. During Puritanical times, there were even laws that made idling a crime punishable by law, not just by God.

I'm no Puritan. I adore idling, Doing Nothing. Laziness is a desirable quality, in my mind. I am not a proponent of uber-productivity, of cramming every minute of the day with productive activities.

Far from it. Some of my favorite activities are purposefully idle: eating a great meal slowly, taking long walks, lounging in bed with my wife Eva, watching movies, reading a good novel, cuddling with my kids, taking naps. Ah, I love naps!

And so procrastination is not inherently evil.

It can be good to procrastinate if you are burned out and need rest, if you go and do something enjoyable with a loved one, if you find solitude and enjoy it, if you go for a walk and sort things out in your head, if you call a friend and have a great conversation, if you have an excellent cup of tea . . .

The list can go on and on.

Procrastination can help us find space, to work at a more leisurely and sane rate, to think and contemplate, to work on our relationships.

But, as I stressed in the last chapter, procrastination can also hurt us in various ways—especially in keeping us from achieving our dreams. So while I would never try to banish procrastination completely, don't use this chapter as justification for procrastinating all day long, every day.

Why We Procrastinate

Let's take a quick look at what makes us procrastinate. There are several usual reasons, which are related in various ways:

We want instant gratification. Resting on the couch is thought of as nicer, right now, than going on a run. Reading blogs is easier, right now, than reading a classic novel, and gives us much quicker enjoyment. Checking email or Facebook is easier, now, than doing that project you've been putting off, and getting a new email or post from a friend is instantly rewarding. Eating chocolate cake is tastier, right now, than eating veggies.

We fear / dread something. We might not write that chapter in our book because there are problems with the writing that we haven't figured out (often because we haven't thought it through). Or we might be afraid we're going to fail, or look ignorant or stupid. We're most often afraid of the unknown, which has more power because we don't examine this fear—it just lurks in the back of our minds. Dreading or fearing something makes us want to put it off, to postpone even thinking about it, and to do something easy and safe instead. See the chapter on Fear and Procrastination for more.

It's easy—no negative consequences right now. When we were in school and had a teacher looking over our shoulders and scolding us if we didn't do our work, we tended to do the work (until some of us learned that we could tune out the scolding, that is). But when we got home, sometimes no one would be looking over our shoulders . . . so there wasn't any immediate negative consequence to watching TV or playing games instead. Sure, we'd get a bad grade tomorrow, but that's not right now. The same is true of using the Internet or doing other kinds of procrastination tasks—we'll pay for it later, but right now, no one is getting mad at us.

We overestimate our future self. We often have a long list of things we plan to do, because we think we can do a lot in the future. The reality is usually a little worse than we expected, but that doesn't stop us from thinking the future will be different yet again. For the same reason, we think it's OK to procrastinate, because we're going to do it later, for sure. Our future self will be incredibly productive and focused! Except, our future self is also lazy—just as much as our current self is, surprise!—and doesn't do it either. Damn future self.

We're not motivated. Procrastination can be our way of telling ourselves that we don't really want to do something. Perhaps we're not excited by it, perhaps we're actually dreading it, perhaps we haven't fully thought out why we want to do this in the first place. Motivation and procrastination are inversely related—to beat procrastination all we often have to do is motivate ourselves. See the chapter Fine-tune Your Motivation.

Inertia. Starting something can be difficult, especially if you know something is good for you but don't have a compelling reason to make the change. It might be that you prefer what you're doing (work vs. exercise, for example). I'd suggest either ditching the goal if you don't want it that badly . . . or increase motivation (see the chapter, Fine-Tune Your Motivation).

A Simple Method

This method works for me every time. Honestly, it hasn't failed once when I decide to apply it.

And that's the key—decide to apply this simple method. When you are conscious about it, it won't fail. It's when we let procrastination happen without thinking that we get beat.

Most of these steps are covered in more detail in other chapters. This chapter is simply to outline the no-fail method.

Choose an important task. And be sure you really, really, really want to do it. Find something about it that excites you. Seriously—don't skip this step. For how to choose an important task, see the next two chapters: Fine-tune Your Motivation, and Choosing Important Tasks.

Make it the first thing you do today, before checking email or anything else. See the chapter called Find Your Best Time.

Keep things simple—don't mess with tools, formatting, anything, just start. Clear away everything that stands in the way of doing. Including turning off the Internet. See the chapter called Create a Distraction-free Workspace.

Just get started. Overcome the initial barrier by diving in. Tell yourself you're just going to do 10 minutes. Forget about perfection. Just start doing it, and fix it later. See the chapters on Single-tasking and The Art of the Small.

Reward your 10 minutes of work with a few minutes of doing something you enjoy—have a cup of tea, stretch and go for a walk, check Facebook or your news sites, whatever you like. Put a timer on this 3–5 minute reward, or it can stretch to an hour!

If you keep procrastinating, re-evaluate whether you really want to do it. Consider not doing it, or putting it on the back-burner.

If all else fails, just take a nap or go outside and enjoy the outdoors or do nothing. Life isn't all about productivity. Do less.

Fine-Tune Your Motivation

Motivation vs. Procrastination. It's the great battle of the workplace, of getting anything done in our lives in general. If we're unmotivated, we'll procrastinate. If we find our motivation, we will beat procrastination. It's often that simple (the exception is when it comes to fear—see the chapter on Fear and Procrastination for more).

If you procrastinate on a task or project, often this is a sign that you aren't that motivated to do it. That might sound obvious, but it's surprising how many people realize this but don't do anything to increase their motivation.

The first question to ask yourself is: Do you really want to do this?

Sometimes, you might surprise yourself—you might realize this is something you don't really want to do. Then ask yourself: can you get away with not doing it? Is it something that absolutely must be done?

Next: Is there something important you really want to do instead?

Is there something that excites you more?

You might consider picking that task to do instead, and killing or postponing the task you don't want to do.

Either way, find a task that's both important to you, and that excites you. This is a task you're motivated to do. Ask yourself why you're excited—what do you envision happening? Is it because of the task itself (it's something you enjoy) or is it what will happen as a result?

It's good to think through these questions—they help you to figure out your motivation and why you're procrastinating.

Make Yourself Accountable

Once you've picked something you're excited about, get some accountability.

Public accountability can be a great motivator. If you can tell someone you're going to do something, you have motivation to get it done. If you tell a group of people, that's even better. Telling the world about it, via your blog or email or Facebook, is the best—it's incredibly motivating to know that people are watching you. Be sure to tell them when you're going to give them an update.

As an example: say you're going to write a book. If you tell no one, you can fail and no one will care. If you tell everyone, you're going to want to write the book. Tell them you're going to give them daily updates, and you'll be motivated to write something every day, just so you can have something good to tell people.

Choosing Important Tasks

Often we procrastinate on the big tasks by doing small tasks. That helps us to feel productive, but in reality we can get a million little things done and not really have anything to show for it at the end of the day.

On the other hand, if you get a few important tasks done, you can call it a day and still feel like you really accomplished something.

Important tasks are the key to how I've gotten so much accomplished, while still having a sane life. I focus on the big tasks, and let the little ones go.

How to Choose

OK, you're convinced that you need to choose important tasks, but how do you choose? You have a long list of things to do but don't know where to start.

There's no right answer. I generally recommend going with whatever excites you most, or with whatever you think will have the biggest impact on your work and life. Either of these is great—if you can find something that fits both criteria, that's perfection.

The amount of impact something will have on your life is very important. You can do a task that will have very little effect on things, or something that will bring you recognition, new customers, huge satisfaction, make your wife love you more . . . you get the idea.

Think about your list and which items are routine and have little impact, vs. the tasks that will have a major impact. As a blogger and writer, for example, writing a really useful post or writing a chapter in my next books are examples of high-impact tasks for me.

In the end, there's no one right answer. It's best just to choose something from among your best choices, and go for it. It won't matter that much if you choose one or the other, if you've narrowed things down to a few important tasks. Eventually you're going to do all of them, if you follow the simple method of this book.

Too Many Tasks

What if you have a long list of tasks to do? Narrow things down. Just choose three from your list, and make this your Short List. The rest will be on your Long List, but you don't need to worry about the Long List right now. You're going to focus on the Short List—just three very important tasks.

The smaller tasks will come after you've finished the Short List. This method of splitting your tasks into two lists is a great way of allowing yourself to focus, to stop from getting overwhelmed.

I recommend setting aside some time at the end of your day for the smaller tasks. We all have routine tasks that need to get done, but if we do these early in the day then they're getting in the way of our Short List tasks. Instead, set aside an hour (or whatever you need) for getting the routine stuff done.

Find Your Best Time

Some times of day are better for getting your important tasks done than others. I love getting things done early in the morning, while Tim Ferriss (of *4-Hour Workweek* and *4-Hour Body* fame) finds late at night to be his most productive time.

There's no one time that works best for everyone. I've tried working late in the evenings, and it didn't work for me: I couldn't focus and ended up doing very little. The rhythms of my body and mind dictate that mornings and early afternoons are the times when I have the most energy

If you don't know your best time for getting important tasks done, experiment. Some ideas:

Try waking a little earlier—10 minutes a day earlier until you're eventually up 40–60 minutes earlier than normal. See if you can make a cup of coffee or tea and get started with your most important task before doing anything else (including checking email or social networks, etc.). Set your most important task the night before.

Try blocking off time as soon as you get to work. So one hour at the beginning of your workday, clear all distractions, don't start email or anything else, and start on your most important task. Set this task at the end of the day before.

Try blocking off time before lunch, or just after. See which works better.

Try a block of time later in the afternoon, or early evening.

Try blocking off time at the end of your day, at night, before you go to bed.

It might take some time, but give each experiment a week and give it your best effort. Believe that it could really work, instead of being dubious. If it doesn't work, at least you gave it your best shot.

I've found that earlier in the day works out best, because as the day goes on things tend to come up that are urgent or that interrupt our plans, and then the important tasks get pushed back further and further, until you put it off to the next day. If you do the important tasks in the first possible time slot (whenever that is for you), you can check it off before your day gets too crazy.

Once you find the time(s) that works for you, make the most of it! Don't schedule anything at this time if possible, and block it off as an uninterruptible appointment to do your important work. Before the time block, prepare: set up the task(s) you want to do, clear your desk and computer, turn off the phones and notifications.

Don't squander your best time!

Create a Distraction-free Workspace

First, a word of caution: procrastinators will use the advice in this chapter as an excuse to procrastinate by fiddling with or overhauling their workspace.

"I'll get to my Important Task as soon as I'm done clearing my desk and downloading the latest distraction-free software!"

No. Don't let the advice in this chapter get in the way of Doing. Setting up the perfect distraction-free environment is not necessary to get to Doing. Here's what I recommend:

Start by clearing anything that might distract you as quickly as possible. Do this before your block of distraction-free work time even starts (if you're going to start at 8:00 A.M., do this 15 minutes before 8:00). Clear everything off your desk and put it on the floor or in a box for now. You can sort through it later. Clear all the icons on your desktop into a new folder in your Documents folder, and sort them out later. Turn off notifications and close your browser if you can get away with not using it during your focus time. Turn off the cell phone and/or mobile device. That's good enough for now.

After, and only after, you've gotten some distraction-free work done, tackle your workspace clutter one thing at a time, maybe doing it in 30-minute chunks once a day until you have a nice clutter-free workspace.

If you can't follow that plan, get away and go to the library or a coffee/tea shop that has no Internet. Plug in some earphones, play some music and get to work.

Declutter Your Desk

Create a beautifully clear desk:

Gather up all your papers. Do you have papers all over your desk? How about stacked on your floor? Gather these all up into one pile, and process them one at a time. This may take awhile if you have a lot of papers, but trust me, it's time well spent. Most of these papers can be trashed, but the important ones need to be filed, with important dates entered in your calendar and actions in your to-do list. File the papers right away. Feel free to toss without mercy, or forward to the appropriate party. Work your way down the stack, starting from the first document. Take one document at a time, make a decision about how to dispose of it, and do it quickly. Don't put it back to decide on later. Don't make several stacks. Do them one at a time, right away. Feel free, though, to do this in 20–30 minute chunks for several days.

Edit your walls. Look at all the stuff on the walls around you. What really needs to be there? Chances are, none of it. We put stuff up on the walls to remind ourselves of things, to inspire ourselves, to make ourselves laugh. But it just distracts us. Take it all down, except perhaps for a nice picture (art is good if you have any), and maybe a nice calendar. If you have a sign to remind you to do a goal or habit, leave that up. I once had a little sign taped to my computer that says, "DO IT NOW" in big blue letters. It was a distraction that distracted me from my other distractions.

Edit your knickknacks. Do you have a bunch of little things on your desk? Photos, cute little animals, candy trays, stuff for pens and paper clips, little signs with funny sayings on them. Get rid of all of them but maybe one or two photos. Pens and paper clips and the like can be put in a desk drawer, neatly in a drawer tray. Most of the other stuff can be tossed, or filed appropriately. This stuff is pure distraction.

Find other spaces for things. If there are things within sight that you need, find a place out of sight for them. Really, there's nothing that needs to be on your desktop (besides an Inbox and your electronic equipment like phone and monitor). Everything else can be put in a drawer. The key: find a place for things, and always put them there. That way, they will be easy to find when you need them. Put the things you use most in the drawers closest to you.

Edit your drawers. Do this on later days, when you have some spare time. Go through drawers one at a time, tossing junk and only keeping what's needed. Organize it, have a place for everything, and make sure you always put stuff back in its place.

Edit your filing system. Do you file your documents regularly? Can you find it immediately at any time? If so, you're ahead of the game. If not, get into the habit of filing things right away. Don't have a "To File" pile—just file stuff right away! Your filing drawer(s) should be close at hand so there's no reason not to file something immediately or pull the file if you need it. Or do as I did, eventually, and go paperless.

Declutter Digitally

If you use your computer as your main work tool, as I do, you'll want to clear it of distractions:

Edit your computer. Most people have a desktop cluttered with icons. This is distracting, and it's hard to find stuff. In my My Documents folder, I created four folders: 1. Inbox 2. Working 3. Read and 4. Archive. I download everything to

1. Inbox, and try to clear it out at least daily. I work mostly in the 2. Working folder. The other two are self-explanatory. So take everything on your desktop and file it. If there are actions that you need to do, put them in Working. If there are programs or files you need to access regularly, you can put them in your Start menu or Dock (or equivalent), or even better, use *Launchbar* or develop an *Autohotkey* for it. Then turn off your desktop icons, and get a nice serene desktop pic.

No Internet. If you can get away with doing your Important Tasks without the Internet, absolutely do it. Close your browser if at all possible. Shut off the Internet if you can. Go to a place with no Internet access if necessary. If you need to do research on the Internet, do it before your block of distraction-free time, and save the research so you don't need the Internet when you do your Important Tasks. Use an Internet blocker like *Freedom* if necessary.

No notifications. Turn off any notifications that would pop up while you're trying to focus. Notifications for Facebook, Twitter, new emails, instant messaging, calendar events, etc.

One program. Don't have a bunch of programs open at once. Work on one task at a time, and only have the window(s) open that you need to work on that task.

Use Simple Tools

Some people need complex software such as InDesign or Photoshop or music or video production software. But often we don't—if you're writing something, for example, you can use a plain text editor (*vim, TextWrangler, TextEdit, NotePad*) or a distraction-free editor (*WriteRoom, OmmWriter, Q10*).

Or use pen and paper if you can—they're free of all distractions and work great.

Don't fiddle with your tools. There's no need to get the perfect text editor or the perfect notebook or pen. Those are excuses for procrastination. Use simple tools, but use what you have right now and don't get caught up in perfect.

Single-tasking

The best way to plow through an important task is to single-task. While we've long been trained to be multi-taskers, the truth is our brain can really only focus on one thing at a time, and switching between tasks costs us our focus.

Really focusing on one task means you're giving it your best—your productivity increases, the quality of work increases, and you're happier doing it.

While a few years ago I couldn't sit down to work on something without quickly switching to email or one of my favorite Internet forums or sites, today I can sit down and write. I can clear away distractions, when I set my mind to it, and do one thing. And that changes everything: you lose yourself in that task, become so immersed that you pour everything you have into the work, and it becomes a meditative, transformative experience. Your happiness increases, stress goes down, and work improves.

We're going to look at single-tasking best practices, and how to increase your ability to single-task if you're not good at it (and most people aren't).

Single-tasking Best Practices

Many of these best practices are covered elsewhere, but briefly:

Close the browser and your email program. If you need to work in the browser then make sure no tabs or windows are open other than the one you absolutely need.

Turn off all notifications.

Turn off the Internet. Shut off your connection, unplug your router, or best yet, go to a place where there is no Internet (yes, those still exist).

Close all programs and windows other than what you need for this one task.

Have a very important task to do.

Clear your desk.

Plug in the headphones (optional).

Once you have this environment (and you shouldn't spend more than a few minutes setting it up), get going on your task. Do nothing but that one task. Don't switch to another task. Having trouble doing that? Read on.

How to Increase Your Single-tasking Abilities

If you can't focus on one task for very long, don't worry. That's normal. Our brains have been trained by technology and society to switch tasks often.

One way we've been trained is that switching to check email or blog updates or Facebook/Twitter is rewarding—we are rewarded with a little nugget of satisfaction in that someone has sent us a message (social validation!) or we have something new and interesting to read (shiny and bright!). Switching tasks becomes a positive feedback cycle that is hard to beat by single-tasking.

The way to beat that is to set up a positive feedback cycle for focusing. Here's how:

Start small. You only need to single-task for one minute at first. Clear everything away, pick your one important task, and just do it for one minute without switching. This is hard to do in the beginning but if you consciously focus on it, you can do it. It's just a minute.

Reward yourself. The reward for single-tasking for one minute can be one minute (or 30 seconds) of checking whatever you want. Email, Facebook, whatever. Or get up and take a one-minute walk. Stretch, drink some water, massage your neck, enjoy your small victory. Empires are created with small victories.

Repeat. Keep doing one minute single-tasking, one minute reward (or 1 minute to 30 seconds if you like) for about half an hour (15 of each). You're done. Repeat that later in the day. Rejoice in how much work you got done! You've set up a positive feedback cycle for single-tasking.

Note: If you feel stressed while single-tasking, which can happen if you're out of your comfort zone, that's OK. Get up, take a deep breath, shake your legs and arms out a bit, stretch, maybe walk around for a minute, then refocus yourself. The stress is normal, and movement can help.

Increase in small steps. Tomorrow, make it two minutes on, one minute off. Repeat that for 30 minutes, do it later in the day too. Feel free to go wild and do three single-tasking sessions in a day, but it's not necessary.

Keep taking baby steps. I think you can see the pattern. Make it three minutes on, one minute off on the third day, then 4:1, then 5:1. When you get to 10 minutes, be crazy and take a 2 minute break. When you get to 20 minutes, take a 3 minute break. At 30 minutes of single-tasking, you've earned a 5 minute break. And once you're at 30 minutes, you can stay there. No need to become a monk.

Set up a positive feedback cycle for single-tasking focus and you'll reverse the years of training your mind has gotten to switch tasks. You'll get more important work done, and it won't seem hard. You'll find that focus becomes a form of meditation. It's a beautiful, beautiful thing.

The Art of the Small

Small is better when it comes to getting to completion. It's easier, which is less friction. It's less intimidating.

But more than that, small tasks and projects are victories. You can quickly get to completion and feel great about it. And that compels you to keep going.

For example, when I launched my minimalism blog, *mnmlist,* it took three days. One day to buy the domain, set up WordPress, and find a theme to start from. Another day to tweak the theme to what I wanted and write a few posts. A third day to write more posts and announce it on Twitter and *Zen Habits.*

Three days, and I was at Done. And getting it public was a big motivator, making it exciting and making me want to work quickly and get to completion.

It doesn't work this way with large projects. Writing a book, for example, often takes at least six months or even more than a year. Which makes it incredibly difficult, so many writers fail. Lots of large projects work this way—they're hard to finish, hard to motivate yourself, hard to stay excited about.

A couple other examples: I wrote my latest book, called *Focus,* by writing it in small chunks (I call them beta versions) and making it public. Each version was a small project, but they could all be done quickly. Also, I released the theme of mnmlist by tweaking the theme I was using and making it ready for release, in just one day. Quickly got to done, and released it to the public. It was satisfying.

I wrote this book on procrastination in just a few days by breaking it into small chapters and writing each chapter quickly in a distraction-free space.

Keeping tasks and projects small means they have less friction, and it's easier to stay motivated. Keep things simple. Narrow your focus. Do less, have less features, offer less services. Small is better, because you'll get to completion.

Fear and Procrastination

The biggest reason people procrastinate is because of some unspoken fear. If we can summon the courage to even take a look at these fears, we've gone a long way toward beating procrastination.

Fear is something that lurks in the darkness, something we often don't even acknowledge exists, something that acts on us in very powerful ways.

We must face these fears, bring them from the unspoken realm to the land of consciousness. And ultimately, we must bring light upon them and, in doing so, strip them of their power.

If you read no other chapter in this book, I ask that you read this chapter, carefully. It is the most important chapter of all, and if you skip over it you can't say you've made your best effort to conquer procrastination. Make your best effort! Truly pour yourself into this battle, and to do so, you have to face your fears, give them names, and take away their power.

Complete the steps in this chapter to get the most of the money you spent on this book, and more importantly to get the most out of your life.

The Fears that Cause Procrastination

There are a litany of fears that plague us, and I can't be exhaustive, but here are some of the most common (and there's a lot of overlap among these fears):

Fear of the unknown. If we're taking on a project that we're not already very good at, it is scary—there is so much we don't know how to do, and it requires courage to face this unknown.

Fear of being overwhelmed. You have so much to do, you don't know where to start, and you're afraid of tackling so much.

Fear of too much work. When you know that a task is going to be very difficult, it is scary, and you'll often put it off.

Fear of missing out. You might not be afraid of a specific task or project, but you keep switching from it to other things (news, social networks, email, etc.) because you're afraid you will miss something important. You don't want to miss an urgent message, or seem dumb because you missed important news, so you allow yourself to get distracted.

Fear of failure. A big one, that encompasses a lot of fears: the fear of not being prepared enough, the fear of failing in your performance, fear that you'll do well but then as a result be put in a position you can't handle.

Fear of looking stupid. This is a variety on the fear of failure, and we all have it. You don't want to do something (like write a book, make a public statement, give a presentation, etc.) and look stupid in front of others. So you avoid it. Sometimes you're afraid of asking for help, because then you'll look stupid for not knowing.

Fear it will take too much time. You anticipate that the time you'll need to focus or be productive will be great—and you dread it or worry that you can't spare that much time.

Fear of too much choice. Choice seems like a good thing but having too many choices can be overwhelming . . . and the fear of making the wrong choice can stop us in our tracks. See the chapter called "Kill Choice" for more.

Steps to Beating Your Fears

Now that you're a bit familiar with some of the common fears, do any of them sound familiar? You might have a fear that's not covered here—that's OK, the steps for beating any fear is pretty much the same.

I urge you to give these steps a try, and not to skip them because they sound silly or too easy:

Examine the fear. Fears get their power from living in the dark—so shine some light on them. Look at them. Become conscious of them. See if you can give them a name—either one of the names above, or one of your own if I haven't named them. Giving your fears a name makes them known, and less powerful.

Commit to beating the fear. You now know it's there, and you don't like the power it has over your life. Tell yourself that you can beat this. It's true, too: I've done it and so have many other people. Commit yourself to making the effort to beat it.

Do an experiment. Fears exist only because we don't know. We don't know if we'll fail, or if we'll miss out on something important, or if we'll look dumb. So let's beat the fears with information: if we don't know something, we're going to find out. Do a short experiment (it can be for 10 minutes, an hour, or a day) and see what happens. For example, if you're afraid you're going to miss something important if you don't check Facebook or email or your text messages, try it for just 30 minutes or an hour, and see what happens. It's an experiment, not a permanent life change, so it's not so scary—you're doing this in the name of science! See what the results are: did your fear come true or not?

There will be some fears where a 10- or 30- or even 60-minute experiment won't show full results. For example, if you're afraid you're going to fail, you won't know after doing something for just 30 minutes . . . but that's OK. Do it for 30 minutes and see if you've failed yet. If not, keep doing it, and you'll see that by focusing on shorter tasks, the fear hasn't (yet) come true—it's not scary to do the small tasks because you're not failing on those.

Once in awhile the fear will come true in your short experiment. You might, for example, get an important email when you turn off the Internet for 60 minutes. But then ask yourself two things: 1) what are the worst consequences of what happened, and 2) is it a fluke? To answer the second question, give the experiment more tries. See what happens the second time and the third. If the fear keeps coming true, you might need to rethink your approach to solve this obstacle. If it doesn't, try the next step.

Expand the experiment. If the short experiment is successful, give it a couple more tries. Then make it longer—if you did if for 10 minutes then make it 30, if you did it for 30 make it an hour, if you did an hour make it two. If you did it for a few hours try all day. If you did it for a day, try two. See what the results are now.

If your experiments were successful, you're now armed with some powerful information. You now (I hope) have evidence that your fear isn't true. If you feel you haven't yet gotten enough evidence, keep doing experiments until your confidence builds. If you have that confidence, then this chapter is a success.

If you don't adequately commit to facing your fears and doing experiments to make them powerless, you are doing yourself a disservice. It's my hope that you put everything you have into this, and make me look good by beating your fears and procrastination.

Reduce Friction to Get to Done

"Done" is a beautiful word.

It means you've achieved something, no matter how minuscule, a victory in a world filled with defeats. It is a tiny leap of joy in your heart, not only a step towards something wonderful but actually something wonderful itself.

Done means you've won, in a battle against procrastination and distraction and endless boring meetings and the constant requests of others, in the battle against a world conspiring to stop Done from ever happening.

Let's make that battle easier. Let's minimize the friction, all the forces against you, and make Done something easy.

Reduce the friction. Grease the slope towards Done. Then give yourself a small nudge, and you're off.

The Friction

What are the things that stop you from getting to done, from even starting on work sometimes? Let's list a few of bigger culprits:

Being overwhelmed by having too much to do.

Too many distractions, such as reading on the web.

Procrastinating—dreading a task.

Not wanting to do a task because it's boring or hard.

Being intimidated by a large project.

Tools are distracting or tough to use.

Fiddling with tools instead of doing.

Other people, making requests, calling, IM'ing, emailing.

Meetings.

Getting to Done

Given the above list of friction, how can we reduce the friction to get to done? I can't give a solution to every single problem that every single reader faces, except in a general way:

Focus on every single friction, and find a way to reduce or eliminate it.

The more you can do this, the less friction you'll have. And the easier it'll be to get done.

Here are just a few examples (many of them covered in other chapters, but listed here to illustrate how to reduce friction):

Eliminate meetings. As much as possible. They're toxic. Focus on actual work.

Eliminate distractions. Turn off email notifications, Twitter, the Internet in general. Turn off phones except certain hours. Only check email at predesignated times. Clear clutter. Don't dawdle on this, though.

Pick simple tools. Not complicated ones, not ones that have distractions. Best tool for writing? A text editor such as TextEdit or Notepad. See the chapter on Creating a Distraction-free Workspace.

Make a task really small. Small is not overwhelming or intimidating. It's easy. You can get to done faster. See the chapter, the Art of Small.

Focus on one thing at a time. Having too many things is overwhelming. What can you do right now that matters?

Make a project smaller. Reduce the scope. Have it doable in a few days or a week. Work on the other parts when the first part is done.

Set office hours. Ask people not to interrupt you except at certain times of the day.

Push back smaller tasks. The other things you need to do that interrupt you. Put them in a text file, and do them an hour before you finish working, so they don't get in the way.

Don't work on boring stuff. Find stuff that excites you. If you can't, consider changing jobs. See the chapter called Fine-tune Your Motivation.

Kill Choice

Choice is a fascinating thing. It seems like such a good thing to have, and yet too many choices can paralyze us. The fear of making the wrong choice is devastating.

And today we are overwhelmed by choices—we have more consumer choices than ever before, we have so much information and entertainment to choose from on the Internet, and when it comes to work we have so much freedom and so many options and possible paths to follow that it can seem almost impossible to choose.

This often causes procrastination. When we have too much to read, we put off reading any one thing. When we have too many possible tasks and projects to work on, we put off doing any one of them.

Life is filled with a ridiculous amount of choices, and as a result of this overwhelming array, we put off making these decisions. We float adrift on a sea of choices, unable to pick a path.

The Solution

Kill choice. When we have few choices (or none), we are ironically freed of the burden of choice.

When we have an important article to read in a browser with 10 or 20 tabs open, we put off reading the important article because there are too many other options for this particular moment. But when we close all other tabs but the one article, and have no way to open anything else, we'll read it.

The amazing French novelist Victor Hugo solved this problem of choice over a century ago. He would strip to the buff, and give all his clothes to his butler, and then write in the nude. He couldn't go outside and take advantage of the amazing cafes or bars in Paris. He couldn't receive visitors while buck naked. He could do nothing but write.

Now that's commitment.

You must kill choice to beat it.

How to Kill Choice

First, choose something important. It's a waste of your time to make the effort to kill choice if you don't have something important to do. How can we choose something important when we have too many choices? Usually we can easily pick a handful of important tasks from among our list (3–5 things perhaps). Once you've narrowed it down to 3–5 things, just randomly pick one of them. It doesn't matter which one.

Now prepare in advance of tackling this task, by eliminating all other choices. Your situation will vary, and the solutions for eliminating choice will vary, but here are some examples:

Shut off the Internet or go somewhere where there is no Internet.

Close your browser or all the tabs except the one you need to read or work on.

Give your router and mobile devices to someone else, and tell them not to give it back to you until you're done with this task.

Hide your TV in the closet if it tempts you.

Use a program to block the choices that normally tempt you.

Go to a park or a library without anything else to do but the task you need.

Use pen and paper and get away from your computer.

More Procrastination Remedies

The Simple Method I outlined earlier in this book has always worked for me—when I consciously apply it. But sometimes it's necessary to try other solutions or tricks. This chapter has some of my favorites.

Put something you dread more than the task you want to do at the top of your to-do list—you'll put off doing that by doing the other things on your list. This is called "structured procrastination."

My favorite procrastination hack: 30–10. Set a timer for 30 minutes, and work for 30 minutes straight. Don't stop until the timer goes off! When you're done, you get to do one of your favorite procrastination activities—checking email, reading your favorite blogs, checking Facebook or Twitter. It's your reward. Do it for 10 minutes only, and then go back to your timer. Here's the key: resist all temptation to check email or your blogs (or whatever your reward activity is) until the 30 minutes comes up. You will probably be tempted, but don't give in.

Stop and think. When we allow fears and other such thoughts to go on without really being conscious of them, we procrastinate. When we actually pause and think about those thoughts, we can rationally see that they're wrong. Instant gratification in the form of goofing off or eating junk food can lead to problems later. Fears are overblown and shouldn't stand in our way. Not having negative consequences now doesn't mean there won't be consequences later. Our future self isn't as bad-ass as we like to think. So think about what you're doing, and start to do the more rational thing.

Enjoy the process. When we dread something, we put it off—but instead, if we can learn to enjoy it, it won't be as hard or dreadful. Put yourself in the moment, and enjoy every action. For example, if you want to go out to run, don't think about the hard run ahead, but about putting on your shoes—enjoy the simplicity of that action. Then focus on getting out the door—that's not hard. Then focus on warming up with a fast walk or light jog—that can be nice and enjoyable. Then feel your legs warm up as you start running a little faster, and enjoy the beautiful outdoors. This process can be done with anything, from washing dishes to reading to writing. Enjoy yourself in the moment, without thinking of future things you dread, and the activity can be very pleasant and even fun. And if it is, you won't put it off.

Set up accountability. If no one is looking over our shoulder, we tend to let ourselves slack off. So set up a procrastination-proof environment—find people to hold you accountable. I joined an online fitness challenge this month, for example, so that I'd report my workouts to the forum. I've done the same thing for running, quitting smoking, writing a novel. You can even just use your friends and family on Facebook or email.

Block your future self. Your future self is just as likely to put things off. So block that sucker. Use a program like Freedom to block your Internet access for a predetermined amount of time, so your future self has to actually focus instead of reading blogs. Turn off your cable TV, get rid of the junk food in your house, cut up your credit cards . . . do whatever it takes to make it really hard for your future self to procrastinate or give in to temptation, or at least force your future self to pause and think before he does anything dumb.

Use your calendar. If you have a task that has been loitering on your to-do list for a long time, schedule it for a specific date and time block in your calendar. Promise to work on that item only.

Do the hard task first. Instead of allowing a task to nag at you all day long, promise yourself that you'll do your hardest task first. The rest of the day feels like gravy!

Engineer Habit Change

Beating procrastination requires that we form several new habits—selecting Important Tasks, for example, clearing our schedule and desks to work on these tasks, and Just Starting.

Habit change, as many of us know, is not always easy. I thought I'd share some tips for creating habits in this chapter. Creating solid habits is the best long-term solution to beating procrastination—this way the changes you make as a result of reading this book will stick.

Let's first imagine people walking through freshly fallen snow. The first person to go through the snow has to forge a path through the snow, and it's difficult . . . but others will follow in that path and it gets easier and easier.

Forming a habit is a matter of forging that initial path until it's harder not to take the path. Who wants to forge a new path through the snow?

But let's take that concept a little further: what if you engineered it so that even the initial person forging through the snow would rather take that path than another, because it would be harder not to take the path.

Engineer your habit change so that it's harder not to form the habit?

Why Habit Changes Fail

I think I can safely say that all of us have attempted and failed at creating a new habit or changing an old habit at a few points in our lives. It can be hard to change old ways and create new ones.

The problem is that creating a new habit can be difficult. The reason: negative feedback.

Negative feedback is when we do something, and it is painful, or difficult, or we get criticized, or in some other way get a bad feeling rather than a good one. Difficult exercise, for example, contains inherent negative feedback, as it is more difficult than sitting on the couch. Quitting smoking contains negative feedback, because you suffer withdrawal pains and urges.

Positive feedback, on the other hand, is when you get compliments from friends and family that you look thinner or healthier, or the satisfaction from the number on the scale dropping. It's the encouraging comments I get on my blog. It's the great feeling when finishing a good run or a 5K.

But when the negative feedback makes the habit change difficult, especially in the first few weeks, habit changes often fail. That's because it's easier to quit the habit change than to keep doing the new habit, because of the negative feedback. It's easier to take a puff from a cigarette (and get positive feedback in the form of pleasure) than to suffer withdrawal pains. It's easier to sit on the couch eating potato chips (again, pleasure feedback) than to go out for that run.

Habit changes fail because the negative feedback from doing the new habit outweigh the positive feedback, and it becomes easier not to do the habit.

Engineer the Habit Change

So how do we overcome this problem? Think of it from an engineer's point of view:

When negative feedback outweighs positive feedback, habit change fails.

To make the habit change successful, positive feedback has to outweigh negative feedback.

The solution: increase positive feedback and/or decrease negative feedback until the ratio favors the habit change.

Think of it this way: if you want to take a certain path in the snow, put obstacles along all other paths so that it's difficult to go anywhere but the path you want to take . . . and have the path you want to take shoveled, so that it's easy to take that path.

You can engineer your habit change so that it's harder to quit than to do the habit.

How to Do It

You have four options in your custom engineering solution. In each, I'll give some ideas, but you'll have to come up with ideas of your own to fit whatever habit you're trying to change.

1. *Increase positive feedback for the habit.* Some habits have instant positive feedback, but often the positive feedback is delayed. It takes awhile to lose weight. It takes awhile before your blog starts getting encouraging comments. This delay in positive feedback is what causes many people to fail, because in the crucial first few weeks they are getting mostly positive feedback.

Instead, find ways to have instant positive feedback. The more, the better. Add as many of these (and others you can think of) as possible to increase chances of success. Some examples:

Creating a log or journal of your habit lets you feel satisfied that you're actually doing the habit.

Joining an online forum, where you can receive positive feedback from others going through the same thing. Quit smoking forums or running forums are two examples I've used.

Join a real-world group, such as a book club, a running club, a class, etc., where you can get similar feedback from people.

Reward yourself, early and often. Small rewards are appropriate, but celebrate every little success.

Email or talk to people about your habit change, giving them daily updates. If people expect the daily updates, you will feel motivated to do your habit so you can tell people about it.

Blog about it. If you have a few readers, they will most likely be encouraging.

2. *Decrease negative feedback for the habit.* First you have to list the negative feedback for your habit. For quitting smoking, there are urges and withdrawal pains. For exercise, it can be an exertion, which takes effort and energy. Analyze the negative feedback for your habit, all of them, and see how to decrease them. Some ideas:

For quitting smoking, reduce urges and withdrawal pains with nicotine gum or patches.

For exercise, reduce exertion by only doing a little bit in the beginning.

For eating healthy, reduce the negative taste feedback by eating healthy treats, such as berries, or adding a little bit of good fat or a little salt to make things tastier.

For reducing sweets, reduce urges by eating little treats, such as a bit of dark chocolate, or fruits.

For developing the reading habit, reduce boredom (if that's the problem) by reading exciting and fun books. Thrillers are favorites of mine.

3. *Increase negative feedback for not doing the habit.* You want to make it hard not to do the habit. As hard as humanly possible. So to do that, you need to put all kinds of negative feedback on yourself for not doing the habit. Some ideas:

If you join a forum or a real-world group or give people you know regular updates, or update your blog readers (see ideas in #1 above), you will face the embarrassment of having to tell people you didn't do the challenge.

Get a partner or coach or trainer, or your spouse, to make sure you do the habit, and to nag you if you don't.

If you're trying to develop the reading habit, remove all other temptations.

If you're trying to exercise, get rid of the TV and Internet and make your house uncomfortable, until you do your exercise. Once you exercise, get your cable TV box or Internet modem back from your neighbor who was holding it for you.

If you're trying to quit smoking, tell your kids not to let you smoke.

I'm sure you can think of many others—get creative!

4. *Decrease positive feedback for not doing the habit.* What tempts you not to do your habit today? Give this some thought, and then decrease those positive things. Some ideas:

If you're trying to exercise (a common example), there is often positive feedback from not exercising, because it's relaxing to stay home. So if that's the case, reduce the relaxation at home. Get your spouse or kids to nag you. Get your mom to call you. Remove the cushions from your couch. Be creative!

If you're trying to stop procrastinating, the positive feedback for procrastination is the fun of going on the Internet (for example). Well, disconnect from the Internet or use a utility to block the sites that waste your time.

If you're trying to wake up early, there is of course the positive feedback that comes from sleeping in. Set up multiple alarms all around your room. Have people give you wake-up calls, so you can't sleep. Have people waiting for you at the track for your morning run, or waiting for your phone call for an early business call.

Final word: In the end, be sure that you've engineered it so that it's harder not to do the habit. If you fail, just add more of any or all of the above four options and try again. Don't give up!

Procrastination Questions, Answered

Most of the common questions about procrastination are answered in previous chapters, but here are additional questions readers have asked:

Q: How do I fight the need to stay updated (Twitter, Facebook, email, news, blogs, etc.)? Seeing Twitter has new updates I haven't refreshed yet really pulls me away from work.

A: First realize that this is a fake need, and we don't really need to be updated so much. There was a time when we were only updated with the morning newspaper and evening news—and people survived! Try an experiment—go half a day without being updated and see if your world collapses. What bad things result from the experiment? What good things?

If necessary, use a program like *LeechBlock* to block the sites that you're addicted to, except for certain periods of the day. Give yourself very specific time frames to check the things that pull you away, and stick to that schedule.

Q: Once procrastination is ingrained in your schedule and has become a habit, how do you stop that inertia?

A: Habits are hard to change, but not at all impossible. It takes commitment (you have to really be serious about it) and a very conscious effort. Dedicate yourself for 30 days to doing your Most Important Task at a certain time block each day (say, 8–9 A.M. on weekdays), and tell everyone about it. Commit to giving them daily updates on your habit change, and reward yourself at the end of each focused time block by posting on Facebook or Twitter or your blog about your success that day.

Q: How do I not rely on deadlines as motivation?

A: Deadlines are actually great motivation—someone is waiting for you to finish, so it gives you the motivation to get off your butt and get it done. It puts a little urgency into your work. If you're motivated by deadlines but don't like waiting until the very last minute, try a modified version: set mini-deadlines for smaller parts of the project, and make a commitment to a friend or co-worker to send them the completed parts of the project by those mini- deadlines. That way you are tackling smaller tasks and getting work done in increments without waiting until the last minute.

Q: What's the first step into doing something?

A: The first step is choosing something important and committing to focusing on it and nothing else. Then tell yourself, "I'm just going to do this for 10 minutes." Take that first step and get moving!

Q: *How do I keep momentum going?*

A: Once you've gotten started, think of that as a victory. Feel good about it! Getting a small step done can be a reward in itself. Continue that good feeling by getting another small step done, and then another. Be proud of yourself and tell people about it. Keep going, and rejoice in your progress. Break the project or task into tiny tasks, list them out, and check them off as you go—it can be fun to keep checking things off.

Q: *I have too many things to do and don't know where to begin.*

A: There are two ways to go here. The first is to make a list of things to do (you're taking control), and then choose the most important thing on the list. You might even make a smaller list (a Short List) of your top three things, and forget about the longer list for now—focus on the Short List.

The second approach is to pick the easiest task on the list and get it out of the way. Then the next easiest thing. These are the low-hanging fruit—easiest to pick, so start with them. This is a form of procrastination for many people, but when you're overwhelmed it can feel good to get a few small things done. Once you've got some momentum, do the Short List approach above so you can get to the important things.

Q: *Because of my personality, I can only find motivation under the pressure of a looming deadline. Is that true or just an excuse?*

A: Well, it's true that many of us are motivated by deadlines. It's usually a trait we developed in one or more jobs, or at school. There's nothing wrong with that—use that trait by setting deadlines and committing to them to someone whose opinion you value, or committing to it in public.

However, just because that's how you usually work, doesn't mean that's the only way you can work. If you pick things to work on that you love and are excited about, you can find pleasure in the tasks themselves, and if you focus on that enjoyment, it can be motivating to just dive in and do them, without the need for deadlines. Give it a try!

Q: My problem is the fact that there are always interesting and somehow justifiable things to do whenever the important task at hand gets scary.

A: Yes, that's a common avoidance tactic. We tend not to want to even think about things that we fear, and so we go do other things. Unfortunately, that only gives more power to the fear—and as a result we end up running from the fear all the time instead of being in control of our lives.

Read the chapter on fear. Fear can be beaten easily, but you have to want to do it.

Q: I've given up fighting procrastination, I think. How can I make it work in my favor instead?

A: As I've said in the early chapters, procrastination isn't all bad. It can be a lovely way to enjoy life, to relax and get the rest we need, to re-evaluate our jobs and lives and whether we're doing things we hate. Unfortunately, it can also hurt us. So first think about whether you're being hurt or not.

But . . . you can use procrastination in a positive way. One of my favorites is called Structured Procrastination. Make a list of everything you need to do, and put them in order of importance. Commit to doing the first thing at the top—but if that thing is something you want to put off, do the second thing instead. Feel free to procrastinate on the top thing by doing the things below it. You'll find you get a lot done. What about that thing at the top? Eventually you'll have something you need to do more than that top thing—put that new thing at the top and get the old top thing done instead.

And Done

Congratulations on finishing the book! It feels amazing to complete something, doesn't it?

And thank you for reading.

Leo Babauta

Zen Habits

CPSIA information can be obtained at www.ICGtesting.com
Printed in the USA
BVOW02s1336150514

353487BV00001B/116/P